EARTH'S ENERGY RESOURCES

WATER ENERGY

ELSIE OLSON

Consulting Editor, Diane Craig, M.A./Reading Specialist

An Imprint of Abdo Publishing
abdopublishing.com

abdopublishing.com

Published by Abdo Publishing, a division of ABDO, PO Box 398166, Minneapolis, Minnesota 55439.

Printed in the United States of America, North Mankato, Minnesota

052018
092018

Design and Production: Mighty Media, Inc.
Editor: Liz Salzmann
Cover Photographs: Shutterstock
Interior Photographs: iStockphoto, Library of Congress, Shutterstock, Wikimedia Commons

Library of Congress Control Number: 2017961704

Publisher's Cataloging-in-Publication Data
Name: Olson, Elsie, author.
Title: Water energy / by Elsie Olson.
Description: Minneapolis, Minnesota : Abdo Publishing, 2019. | Series: Earth's energy resources
Identifiers: ISBN 9781532115578 (lib.bdg.) | ISBN 9781532156298 (ebook)
Subjects: LCSH: Water-power--Juvenile literature. | Power resources--Juvenile literature. | Hydraulic power plants--Juvenile literature. | Energy harvesting--Juvenile literature. | Energy development--Juvenile literature.
Classification: DDC 333.914--dc23

SandCastle™ Level: Fluent

SandCastle™ books are created by a team of professional educators, reading specialists, and content developers around five essential components—phonemic awareness, phonics, vocabulary, text comprehension, and fluency—to assist young readers as they develop reading skills and strategies and increase their general knowledge. All books are written, reviewed, and leveled for guided reading, early reading intervention, and Accelerated Reader™ programs for use in shared, guided, and independent reading and writing activities to support a balanced approach to literacy instruction. The SandCastle™ series has four levels that correspond to early literacy development. The levels are provided to help teachers and parents select appropriate books for young readers.

EMERGING · BEGINNING · TRANSITIONAL · FLUENT

CONTENTS

ALL ABOUT WATER ENERGY

We use energy each day!

It comes from many **sources**.
Water is one source.

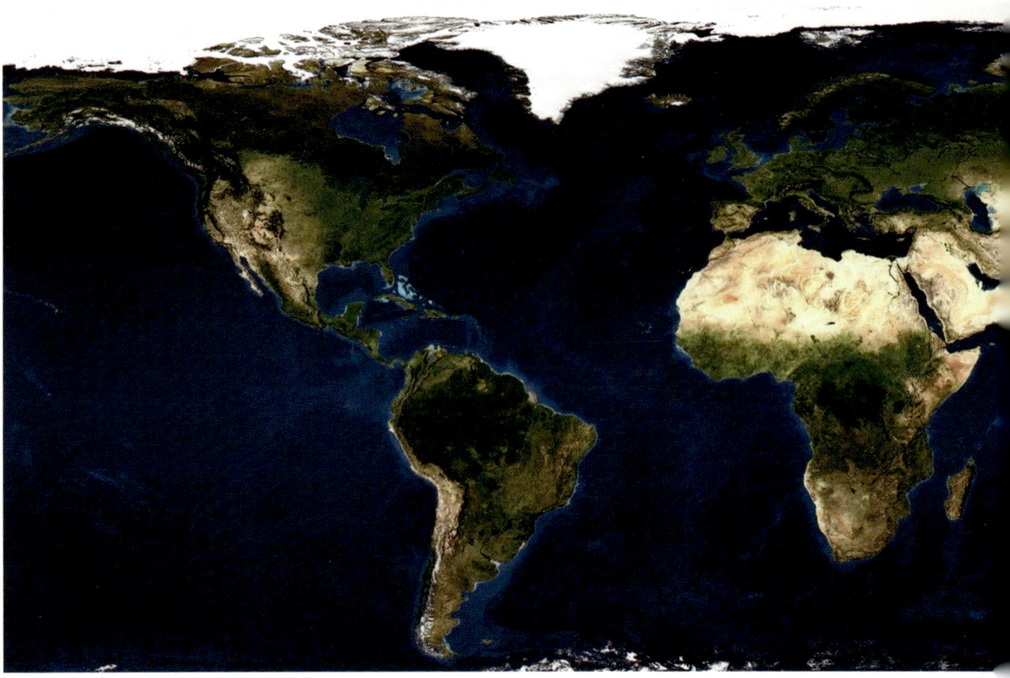

Water covers most of Earth's surface.

Water moves through rivers, streams, and oceans.

Moving water has a lot of energy.

People can use
this energy.

Humans have used water energy for thousands of years.

They first used waterwheels to **grind** grain.

Lester Allan Pelton was an inventor.

He made a better waterwheel. The paddles had a special shape. They got more energy from the water.

Today we use water **turbines** to create electricity.

This happens at power plants.

Moving water turns a **turbine**.
The turbine powers a **generator**.

This makes electricity!

Water is a **renewable resource.**

It doesn't get used up.

Scientists are working on better ways to use water energy.

One day more of our power may come from water energy!

THINK ABOUT IT

In what new ways can we use water energy?

GLOSSARY

generator – a machine that creates electricity.

grind – to crush something into a powder.

renewable – able to be replaced by nature.

resource – something that is usable or valuable.

source – where something comes from or begins.

turbine – a machine that produces power when it is rotated at high speed.